Brant's Little Book

Of

Trivia

Volume   1

Dedicated to my mom and dad, my mawmaw and grandpa, and to trivia lovers everywhere

Telephone

The first phone call was placed on March 10, 1876 when inventor Alexander Graham Bell called his assistant, Thomas Watson, saying "Mr. Watson, come here, I want to see you."

The cost of a telephone in 1876 was around $20- around $431.31 in 2013.

Rutherford B. Hayes was the first president to have a telephone installed in the white house. His phone number? #1

Alexander Graham Bell could never have a phone call with his wife or mother. Both were deaf.

Alexander Graham Bell wanted the traditional phone greeting to be 'ahoy'. Thomas Edison later suggested 'hello'.

When Alexander Graham Bell died in 1922, the USA and Canada paid homage by shutting down all phone calls for 1 minute, affecting over 21,000,000 calls.

Originally, push-button telephones had only 10 buttons. The # and * buttons came in 1968.

The world record for longest phone call was set in 2012 at 46 hours, 16 minutes, 52 seconds.

The Simpsons

In the opening scene, Maggie used to ring up on the grocery store's cash register as $847.63- the estimated cost of raising a baby for one month in 1989.

The phone number Bart uses to call Moe's Tavern is 764-84377.

The French translation for Homer's "D'oh!" is "T'oh!", though in Spanish it translates to "Ouch!"

Comic book Guy's real name is Jeff Albertson.

Bart's locker combination at Springfield Elementary is 36-24-26, the same numbers recited in AC/DC's song 'Dirty Deeds Done Dirt Cheap'.

According to a map found inside the police station, Springfield is shaped like medieval Constantinople.

Krusty the Clown was based off a TV clown creator Matt Groeing watched as a kid named Rusty Nails.

Over 600 celebrities have made cameos on the show, including: Michael Jackson, Sting, Adam West, Hugh Hefner, Meryl Streep, Paul McCartney, Rodney Dangerfield, Mark Hamill, Britney Spears, Stephen King, 50 Cent, Katy Perry (who is the only live-action celebrity to make a cameo), Mark Zuckerberg, Leonard Nemoy, and Stan Lee.

The only character to have five fingers on his hand is God.

State Capitals

Baton Rouge (capital of Louisiana) is French for 'Red Stick'.

The smallest state capital by population is Montpelier, Vermont. It had a population of 7,855 in 2010.

The only state capital to host a summer Olympic Games was Atlanta in 1996.

The only state capital to host a *winter* Olympic Games was Salt Lake City in 2002.

Only 16 out of 50 state capitals (32%) are the largest city of their state.

Salt Lake City, Utah is the only US capital with three words in it. It is also the only state with a chemical compound in it (salt).

Charleston, West Virginia was the site of Summers Street, the first paved brick road in 1870.

Montpelier, Vermont is the only state capital without a McDonalds.

Cheyenne, Wyoming created the world's first yellow pages in 1883 when a printer ran out of white paper and began to use yellow paper while printing a telephone directory.

The heating system at the state capitol building in Denver, Colorado is heated using geothermal energy.

Oklahoma City, Oklahoma had the world's first parking meter installed on July 16, 1935.

Bismarck, North Dakota was named for the German chancellor Otto Van Bismarck.

Crossword Puzzles

The world's first crossword puzzle (then called "word-crosses") was published on December 21, 1913 in the *Sunday New York World.*

During World War 2, Britain's decryption establishment, Bletchley Park, asked cryptologists to solve a Daily Telegraph crossword in under 12 minutes as part of its recruitment process.

Cruciverbalism is the term for creating crossword puzzles.

Crossword writers at the *New York Times* are paid $200 for a weekly puzzle and $1,000 for a Sunday puzzle.

The world's largest crossword puzzle has 28,000 clues for over

91,000 squares. Its clue book is over 100 pages long.

A version of a crossword puzzle has been found inscribed on an ancient tomb in Egypt.

Dick Simon and Lincoln Schuster created the world's first crossword puzzle book in 1924.

The New York Times was one of the last newspapers to officially carry crossword puzzles. They finally released a Sunday edition in 1942 and installed daily puzzles in 1950.

In Japan, the corner squares of all crossword puzzles must be white.

The first crossword puzzle was actually not in the shape of square, but was rather in the shape of a diamond.

Slavery

The first person to legally own a slave in what would become the USA, Anthony Johnson, was black.

The Holy Bible does not condone or forbid slavery. In fact, Jesus healed a slave and condoned his master for his faith.

Slaves in the past could cost upwards of $40,000 in today's money, while the average slave today sells for only $90 on average.

Harriet Tubman never lost a single slave on any of her 19 trips on the Underground Railroad. One of her famous tricks was drugging children with opium to keep them from crying.

The Romans had a yearly celebration day where the roles of slave and master were reversed.

The first foreigner to become a samurai in Japan was an African slave.

U.S. president James Buchanan regularly bought slaves in Washington, D.C. and would later release them in Pennsylvania.

It is reported that there are more slaves in the world today than during the slave trade, despite the fact that it is illegal in every country in the world.

Aesop, the man famous for his fables, was once a Greek slave, though he was later freed for his wit and stories and became a delegate for Greece.

Palindromes

Palindromes are words or phrases that are spelled the same way forwards and backwards, like kayak. Here are a few interesting ones:

Madam I'm Adam

Never odd or even

Saippuakauppias

Yo banana boy

Natasha lived as a devil. Ah, Satan

Rats live on no evil star

Evil olive

Go hang a salami, I'm a lasagna hog

Dana died in ad

A santa at NASA

UFO tofu

A nut for a jar of tuna

As I pee, sir, I see Pisa

Delia saw I was ailed

Drab as a fool, aloof as a bard

Dennis and Edna sinned

Do good? I? No! Evil anon I deliver. I maim nine mire hero-men in Saginaw, sanitary sword a-tuck, Carol, I—lo!—rack, cut a drowsy rat in Aswan. I gas nine more hero-men in Maimi, Reviled, I (Nona) live on. I do, O God!

Draw, O coward!

Eva, can I stab bats in a cave?

Lepers repel

Lonely Tylenol

Ma is a nun, as I am

Coca- Cola

Coca-Cola has over 3,500 soft drinks in its arsenal. If you wanted to try them all, at a rate of one a day, it would take you over 9 years.

Coke drinkers are, on average, more likely to have graduated college than Pepsi drinkers.

You can buy a coke in every country in the world, except Cuba and North Korea.

In 1985, Coca-Cola became the first soda in space.

Coca-Cola is the 2nd most widely understood term in the world, just after 'ok'.

The first celebrity endorsements for Coca-Cola were singer Hilda Clark and opera-star Lillian Nordica.

The Chinese name for Coca-Cola once translated to "Wax-Fastened Female Horse".

Coca-Cola was originally marketed as a nerve tonic that could cure morphine addiction and male impotence.

Three people have tried to sell coke's secret ingredient to Pepsi, but Pepsi reported all of them to Coke and the FBI.

3.1% of all beverages consumed in the world every day are coke products.

There are 33 non-alcoholic brands that generate over $1 billion annually, and coke owns 15 of them.

A can of Diet Coke will float in water while a can of regular coke will sink.

Band-Aids

The first Band-Aid was created in 1920 because Johnson & Johnson employee Earle Dickson's wife Josephine was very accident prone and kept cutting herself while making dinner.

Band-Aids made only $3,000 in their first year, and were only made successful after they were supplied to the Boy Scouts of America.

When they were first released on the market, Band-Aids sold for only 5 cents.

The first decorative Band-Aids, featuring Stars N' Stripes, came out in 1951.

The jingle "I'm Stuck on a Band-Aid" was written by Barry Manilow.

The Band-Aid manufacturing plant is based in North Brunswick, New Jersey.

Band-Aids went into space in 1963 with the Mercury astronauts.

Band-Aids did not become completely sterilized until 1939, just in time for World War 2.

Earle Dickson, mentioned above, was later promoted to Vice President of Johnson & Johnson, which he held until his retirement in 1957.

The original Band-Aids were 2 ½ inches wide by 18 inches long.

At the time of Earle Dickson's death in 1961, Johnson & Johnson was selling over $30,000,000 worth of Band-Aids each year.

Judo

Judo, in Japanese, means "the gentle way".

Judo was the first martial art accepted at the Olympic Games, n 1964.

Judo players are officially called "judokas".

The sport was developed by Jigoro Kano in 1882 as a less violent form of jujitsu.

Judo was first introduced to the US in 1902, and became regulated by the Amateur Athletic Union in 1952.

Women's Judo was introduced to the Olympics in 1992.

James Bond preformed a Judo fight in the 1964 film "Goldfinger".

Judo is the only Olympic sport where choking and breaking your opponent's arm is legal.

According to the official rule book, Judokas must "be clean and have dry skin and short finger nails and toe nails." It also states that Judokas must "be free of any body odor."

More people practice Judo in France than in Japan.

Judo is the most practiced martial art on the planet, and the second most practiced sport, just behind soccer.

Tickets for the Judo competition were the first to sell out for the 2000 Sydney Olympics.

The Japanese police force has practice Judo since 1886.

Television

The first TV broadcast in history was broadcasted in 1936.

The first pianist to perform a recital on TV, Earl Wild, was also the first person to stream a recital on the internet, 60 years later.

People who grew up watching black and white television would often dream in black and white.

The Today Show first went on air on January 16, 1956.

The Wizard of Oz did not become financially successful until it appeared on TV in 1956, as most of the audience at the movie theaters were children who paid a reduced rate.

The first TV commercial aired on NBC in 1941. It was a 60- second ad for Bulova clocks- which the Bulova clock company paid $9 for.

The cost of a 30-second ad during the 2014 Super Bowl was $4,000,000.

The most watched series finale in US history was for M*A*S*H's finale titled "Goodbye, Farewell, and Amen". It aired in 1983 and was watched by over 105.9 million people.

The first couple shown in bed together on television was Fred and Wilma Flintstone.

Until 1987, there were no TV programs broadcast on Thursdays in Iceland.

The United Nations

Franklin Delano Roosevelt proposed the name of the United Nations to British Prime Minister Winston Churchill while Churchill was in a white house bath tub.

While the UN headquarters is in New York City, the UN isn't considered part of the US. The UN sits on its own land with its own post office and postage stamps.

Actor Shirley Temple was once a UN representative for the USA.

The UN was founded on October 24, 1945 with 51 original members.

The UN has 193 members, the newest being South Sudan, the youngest country in the world (it was created in 2011).

Between 1948 and 2005, the UN spent over 40 billion dollars on peace keeping.

Israel has violated 69 rules set by the UN and was never punished, while Iraq broke two and was bombed, raided, and destroyed.

The official languages of the UN general assembly are: Arabic, English, French, Mandarin, Russian, and Spanish.

The only permanent members of the UN's Security Council are the US, Russia, Britain, France, and China. The other 10 members are elected every 2 years.

The General Assembly, where the 193 member countries debate, has no power of its own to enforce decisions. It only has the power to make suggestions.

Sherlock Holmes

In the story the seven-percent solution, Sherlock Holmes is treated for a cocaine addiction by Sigmund Freud.

Sir Arthur Conan Doyle, the creator of Sherlock Holmes, also worked as a ship's surgeon, a boxer, a first-class cricketer, and a Deputy Lieutenant.

Sherlock Holmes never said "Elementary my dear Watson."

Sherlock Holmes is the second most portrayed character in film, just behind Dracula.

Sherlock Holmes' original name was Sherrinford.

The first name of Dr. Watson is John- except in one novel. In one novel, his wife refers to him as James.

Doyle killed Sherlock Holmes off after 6 years in the story "The Final Problem" because he wanted to work on other projects. However, public outcry made Doyle write more stories explaining that Sherlock had faked his death.

Doyle once said that if in a hundred years he was only known as the man who created Sherlock Holmes, then he considered his life a failure.

Doyle was friends in real life with magician Harry Houdini.

Dr. Watson's original name was Ormand Sacker.

Sherlock Holmes, like his creator, was a spiritualist and believed in ghosts and fairies.

Fireworks

Americans have been setting off fireworks to celebrate independence since 1777.

The Chinese have used fireworks to scare off mountain men since around the 7th century.

The first recorded firework show in England was at the wedding of King Henry VII in 1486.

The world record for largest firework display consisted of 77,282 fireworks which were set off in Kuwait in 2012.

The Japanese word for fireworks, hanabi, means fire-flower.

Three sparklers burning together generate the same heat as a blow torch.

90% of all fireworks worldwide are created in China.

Blue is the hardest color to create in fireworks, as it is done using copper oxidizers and the temperature has to be just right.

The Walt Disney Company is the largest consumer of fireworks in the US.

Originally, fireworks were only white and orange.

A rocket can reach speeds upward of 150 MPH.

Captain John Smith was the first person to put on a firework show in America.

Around 50% of all firework injuries occur to people under 17.

A firework shell can reach heights of up to 200 meters.

Pizza

There is a pizza place in Alaska that delivers pizza by airplane.

Americans eat an average of 18 acres of pizza every day.

94% of all Americans eat pizza regularly.

The first pizzeria in the US was opened in Chicago in 1903.

36% of Americans consider pizza the perfect breakfast.

Domino's pizza reported a record sales day on the date of the OJ Simpson trial.

One of the most popular pizza toppings in Japan is squid.

The world's largest pizza was made in Norwood Supermarket, South Africa and weighed 12.9 tons.

The world's fastest pizza maker can make 14 pizzas in 2 minutes and 35 seconds.

36% of all pizza orders are for pepperoni.

October is National Pizza Month in the US.

The average American eats 46 pizza slices annually.

Pizza delivery men claim women are better tippers than men.

The least popular pizza topping in the US is anchovies.

The most popular pizza size in the US is 14 inches in diameter.

The most expensive, commercially available pizza costs $1,000 and is topped with caviar, lobster, cremefraiche, and chives.

Benjamin Franklin

Ben Franklin taught himself to read French, Spanish, Latin, and Italian.

In 1751, Ben organized the first insurance company in the colonies. He also created the first volunteer fire company in 1736.

Ben was an excellent swimmer and once swam from Chelsea to Blackfraiars, a distance of about 3.5 miles.

Benjamin Franklin loved to travel and crossed the Atlantic Ocean 8 times in his life. His first trip was when he was 18 and his final trip was when he was 79.

Ben created the first musical instrument created in America, the glass harmonica.

Ben hated the English alphabet, noting the inconsistencies in spelling and redundant letters. His solution? He created his own alphabet, getting rid of the letters c, j, q, w, x, and y.

Ben Franklin created the first known pro and con list.

Ben was one of the children in a family of 17 children.

Ben Franklin created the postal service and served as the first postmaster of Philadelphia.

Ben created the first US coin, named the Fugio coin, in 1787.

Over 20,000 people attended Ben's funeral when he was buried in Christ Church Burial Ground on April 17, 1790.

Atari

Atari's in-house newsletter was called "The Gospel According to St. Pong."

Nolan Bushnell, the founder of Atari, started Atari in 1972 with an investment of $250. Within 5 years, the company was worth $28 million, and within 10 years had annual sales of $2 billion.

Jack Black's first job as an actor was in a commercial advertising Pitfall for the Atari 2600.

Nolan Bushnell, mentioned above, also created Chuck E. Cheese.

Coca-Cola asked Atari to make a 2600 game for its Atlanta employees. The game they made was a recreation of Space Invaders but instead of shooting aliens you shoot the letters P E P S I.

Steve Jobs was fired from the Atari nightshift because he walked around barefoot and never bathed.

The original name for Atari was going to be Syzygy, a term for a planetary alignment, but was changed to Atari when they found Syzygy was already taken.

The Atari 2600 had the first horror game, a game based off the Texas Chainsaw Massacre.

The Atari 2600 also had several "adult" games released on it, most famously a game called "Bachelor Party."

The original price of an Atari 2600 was $199. At that price, it sold over 30 million units.

Pigs

A pig cannot look up, as it has no neck.

In English, pigs say oink-oink, but other cultures and countries use other sounds for them. In French, they say groan-groan, in Russian qrr-qrr, in Japanese boo, and in German crr-cul.

Pigs aren't really dirty animals, they just enjoy rolling in mud to keep themselves cool. Besides that, they are very clean animals.

The pig is the last of the 12 animals in the Chinese zodiac, and is seen to represent fortune, honesty, happiness, and virility.

The average pig is as smart as a three year old human.

Hernando De Soto, the famous Spanish explorer, brought the first pigs to North America in 1539.

An adult pig can drink upwards of 14 gallons of water every day.

Pigs have no sweat glands, so they cannot cool themselves naturally.

The average pig can run a mile in around 7 minutes.

The most money ever paid for a pig was $56,000 for a pure-breed named Bud on March 5, 1985.

Pigs have been used in warfare to sniff for land mines.

Fleas and ticks do not harm pigs as their skin is too thick to bite easily.

An adult pig will have 44 teeth.

The fastest relative of the pig is the warthog which can run at 35 MPH.

Rock 'n' Roll

The first person to use the term rock 'n' roll was Alan Freed, who was a D.J. in Cleveland.

The first rock musical on Broadway was "Hair" which opened in 1968.

The Who has never had a number one record in the US or the UK.

Paul McCartney performed at the 2012 London Olympics Opening Ceremony for $1.57.

The Beatles are the only band to have the entire top 5 billboard hit songs occupied at the same time.

Jimi Hendrix was paid $18,000 for playing at the 1969 Woodstock Festival plus $12,000 for the rights to film him.

AC/DC guitarist Malcolm Young was once employed as a sewing-machine mechanic in a bra factory.

The only member of ZZ Top who does not have a beard is drummer Frank Beard.

The Nirvana song "Smells Like Teen Spirit" is named after a deodorant brand.

The shortest rock song in history lasts 1.316 seconds. The song is called "You Suffer" by Napalm Death and only has one line, "You suffer, but why?"

Termites will eat wood twice as fast when listening to heavy metal.

Led Zeppelin has had 94 albums go platinum- the most of any band.

There are more than 4,000 versions of "Yesterday" by the Beatles.

Star Wars

The only characters that appear in all 6 films are C3P0 and R2-D2.

The original name for the main character was Luke Starkiller.

The original name of the third film "Return of the Jedi" was going to be "Revenge of the Jedi" but was later changed as George Lucas thought that revenge wasn't something a Jedi would seek.

Master Mace Windu is the only Jedi to carry a purple lightsaber in any of the films.

Yoda is the only main character to die of natural causes.

Chewbacca was based on George Lucas' dog Indiana.

"The Empire Strikes Back" is the only Star Wars film that does not include a trip to the planet Tatooine.

The voice of Yoda is provided by Frank Oz, the same man who voices Miss Piggy.

Every Star Wars film has been released in May, always one week after George Lucas' birthday on the 14th.

If you were to build a Death Star in real life, it would cost $15.6 septillion dollars, or 1.4 billion times the US national debt.

George Lucas was diagnosed with hypertension and exhaustion as a result of filming Star Wars.

The Millennium Falcon was inspired by the shape of a hamburger with an olive on the side.

Montana

Montana is the 4th largest state, just behind Alaska, Texas, and California.

Montana has the largest grizzly bear population if the lower 48 states.

The average square mile of land in Montana has an average of 1.4 elk, 1.4 pronghorn antelope, and 3.3 deer.

Montana has the highest number of different mammals of any state in the US.

The Montana Yogo Sapphire is the only gem from North American gem to be included in the Crown Jewels of England.

In 1888 Helena (Montana's capital) had more millionaires per capita than any other city in the world.

You can fit Virginia, Maryland, Delaware, Pennsylvania, New York, and the District of Columbia within Montana's borders.

Montana has the third-lowest population density in the United States.

Nicknames for Montana include the treasure state and big sky country.

The largest snowflake ever recorded fell in Montana on January 28, 1887 and was close to 15 inches wide.

Montana has the largest migratory elk herd in the US.

The Roe River in Montana is the world's shortest river at 200 feet.

Theodore Roosevelt

Theodore Roosevelt was the first president to travel outside the United States. He visited Panama in 1906 to oversee production on the Panama Canal.

Theodore Roosevelt was the first American to receive a Nobel Prize which he got for his role as a negotiator in the Russo-Japanese war in 1906.

Theodore Roosevelt was blinded in his left eye in a boxing match he had while president.

Theodore Roosevelt took a four minute flight on a plane built by the Wright brothers in 1910, making him the first president to fly in an airplane.

Theodore Roosevelt's mother and first wife both died on the same day, Valentine's Day 1884.

Once while giving a speech in 1912, Theodore was shot by a saloon owner. Since he was not coughing up blood, he refused medical treatment until he finished his 90 minute speech, famously saying "It takes more than that to kill a bull moose."

Roosevelt was a prolific author who penned more than 25 books.

Roosevelt was the first person to call the president's home "The White House."

Maxwell House once asked President Roosevelt what he thought of their coffee. His response? "It's good to the very last drop."

Disney

For many years, Walt Disney had the patent for Technicolor, meaning he was the only animator that could make cartoons in color.

Actor Steve Martin once worked in the magic shop at Disneyland.

Walt Disney was presented with one normal sized Oscar and seven miniature Oscars for Snow White and the Seven Dwarves.

Mickey Mouse's original name was Mortimer, but Walt Disney's wife thought Mickey had a better ring to it.

Lilo and Stich features more Elvis songs than any of Elvis Presley's own movies did.

The final film Walt Disney personally oversaw was The Jungle Book.

When President Harry Truman visited Disneyland in 1957, he refused to ride the Dumbo ride as he was a Democrat and elephants are the symbol of the Republican Party.

Aladdin's face was modeled after actor Tom Cruise's.

None of the shops in Disney World sell gum, as Walt Disney thought that gum stuck onto railings would inconvenience visitors.

The Black Cauldron was Disney's first animated to receive a PG rating.

Walt played Peter Pan in a high school play.

Pepsi

Pepsi was originally called "Brad's Drink" by customers, and was later renamed "Pepsi-Cola."

Pepsi actually makes more revenue than Coca-Cola, though the majority of it comes from their other brands such as Gatorade and Frito-Lay.

Pepsi was the first American product to be produced, marketed, and sold in the former Soviet Union.

Pepsi was the first beverage company to introduce 2-liter soda sizes.

Each can of Pepsi has approximately 8 teaspoons of sugar.

Pepsi was banned in India until 1993 because they would not give a list of their ingredients to Indian officials.

Pepsi's slogan "Come alive with Pepsi" translated into Chinese as "Pepsi brings your ancestors back to life."

In exchange for Pepsi products, Russia gave Pepsi 17 submarines, a cruiser, a frigate, and a destroyer. At the time, it was the 7th largest submarine fleet in the world.

Pepsi-Cola is an anagram for Episcopal, a large church across the street from the pharmacy where Pepsi creator Caleb Bradham worked at.

Pepsi was originally marketed as a cure to stomach pains, and an aid in digestion.

Cats

Cats have over 100 vocal chords in their throat.

Female cats tend to be right pawed, while male cats tend to be left pawed.

A cat can jump up to 5 times is own height.

When a cat died in Egypt, the family would show mourning by shaving their eyebrows.

The largest cat litter ever recorded had 19 kittens, 15 of which survived.

The most expensive cat ever cost $50,000 was named Little Nicky and was the clone of an older cat.

The proper term for a cat lover is Ailurophilia, which is a combination of the Greek words for cat and lover.

The first cat show ever organized was put on in London in 1871.

Cats spend nearly 1/3 of their waking time cleaning themselves.

A cat can find its way home from nearly 14 miles away.

The only cat that cannot retract its claws is the Cheetah.

Cats have 230 bones in their body- 24 more than humans.

The scientific term for a hairball is "bezoar."

Cats have 5 toes on their front paws and 4 on their back paws.

Cats officially replaced dogs as the number pet in the USA in 1987.

Cats have 32 muscles in each ear.

McDonald's

McDonald's is the world's largest toy distributor, handing out 1.5 billion toys in Happy Meals every year.

McDonald's sells 75 hamburgers every second.

McDonald's originally sold hot dogs instead of hamburgers.

McDonald's open a new restaurant every 14.5 hours.

It takes the average McDonald's employee 7 months to earn what the CEO makes in an hour.

When McDonald's first opened drive-thrus in China, confused foreigners would get their food from the drive-thru, park their car, and eat inside.

The founder of McDonald's once said that his dream was to have a McDonald's within 10 minutes of every American.

1 out of every 8 Americans has been employed by McDonald's.

The golden arches of McDonald's are recognized by more people than the Christian cross.

McDonald's delivers in 18 countries.

The queen of England owns a McDonald's close to Buckingham Palace.

Ronald McDonald's shoe size is 29 EEE.

Happy Meals first came out in 1979 and cost $1.

There is a ski-through McDonald's in Sweden.

US Currency

The only woman who has appeared on U.S. paper money is Martha Washington who appeared on the $1 silver certificate of 1886 and 1891.

The largest bill ever produced by the US is the $100,000 bill, which had a portrait of Woodrow Wilson on the front.

A mile of pennies laid out is worth $844.80. By that standard, the US is $2.5 million wide.

A three-cent treasury is the smallest amount ever issued on US paper currency. It was released during the Civil War due to a shortage of coins.

Some coins from the past include the half-cent, the two cent, the three cent, and the twenty cent coin.

Pennies that were minted during World War 2 were made with zinc instead of copper, and are actually silver instead of brown.

You have to double fold a piece of US paper currency 4,000 times to get it to tear.

If you have three quarters, four dimes, and four pennies ($1.19), you have the highest amount of money possible without being able to make change for a dollar.

There are 293 ways to make change for a dollar.

The Federal Reserve shreds 7,000 tons (14,000 pounds) of worn out currency every year

Super Bowl

72 footballs are made specifically for the Super Bowl every year.

Every year, over 8 million pounds of guacamole and 14,500 pounds of chips are consumed during the Super Bowl.

The Minnesota Vikings have played in the Super Bowl four times and have not led in the game at any point. They are currently the only team to do so.

The only football teams not to have appeared in the Super Bowl (so far) are The Browns, Jaguars, and Texans.

The average number of people at a Super Bowl party is around 17.

The oldest quarterback to have played in the Super Bowl is John Elway, at 38 years old. The second oldest is Peyton Manning at 37 years 10 months.

The Super Bowl is measured in roman numerals instead of years due to the fact that a football season runs over two calendar years.

The average Super Bowl commercial costs $1,000,000 to produce.

The quarterback who has won the most MVP awards is Joe Montana with three.

The name for the trophy given to the winner of the Super Bowl is the Vince Lombardi Trophy.

Dogs

Dogs have around 1,700 taste buds, while humans have around 9,000 and cats have about 473.

Three dogs survived the sinking of the Titanic, two Pomeranians and a Pekingese.

Young dogs have 28 teeth while adults have 42.

The most popular name for a dog, according to a recent survey, is Max.

The only dog that cannot bark is the Basenji.

When a dog is born, he is blind, deaf, and toothless.

When Lord Byron was told he could not bring his dog to Trinity College, he retaliated by bringing a bear instead.

Spiked dog collars were designed in ancient Greece as a means to protect dogs' necks from wolf attacks.

The name of the dog on the Cracker Jack box is Bingo, and the Taco Bell Chihuahua is a rescued dog named Gidget.

Hollywood's first Dog Star was Rin Tin Tin, a German Shepard who had been wounded in World War one and was adopted by an American soldier. Rin would sign his own contracts with his paw print.

A lost Dachshund was found in the stomach of a giant catfish in Berlin in 2003.

Pineapples

It takes an average of 3 years for a pineapple to mature.

Pineapples are good for colds and coughs.

The world's largest producer of pineapples is said to be Thailand.

One cup of pineapple has between 70 and 85 calories.

Pineapple spread throughout the world due to the fact that sailors kept them on ships to prevent scurvy.

Pineapples are called pineapples because early explorers thought they resembled pine cones.

The top part of a pineapple is called the crown, fitting as the pineapple is nicknamed the King of Fruit.

As soon as pineapples are harvested, they stop ripening.

Pineapple juice mixed with sand is good for cleaning boat decks and machetes.

Unripe pineapples are actually poisonous, causing throat irritation and a strong laxative affect.

Pineapples can weigh upwards of 20 pounds.

Pineapples contain an enzyme that can be used as meat tenderizer.

Males in the Caribbean would run through pineapple plantings as a rite of manhood.

Pineapple plants only produce one pineapple every growing season.

Canned pineapples were first available in 1901.

Burger King

In 2009, Burger King had a special where you would receive a free whopper if you un-friended 10 people from Facebook. The unfriended person would receive a message saying that their friendship was worth less than a whopper.

Burger King's in Australia are called "Hungry Jack's."

Microsoft promoted Windows 7 in Japan by having Japanese Burger Kings sell Whoppers with 7 patties.

In 2008, Burger King sold meat-scented cologne called Flame.

There a 221,184 to mix and match ingredients to create a Whooper.

In 1957, a Whopper cost only 37 cents.

There at least 11 different celebrities who have a lifetime supply of free Burger King Food.

Burger King was originally called Insta Burger King and was opened in Miami in 1954.

90 percent of all Burger King restaurants are independently owned.

Burger King once had a limited time table service promotion that was discontinued after it didn't generate enough interest.

Burger King serves approximately 11.4 million people every day.

After a 13 month year old girl got choked on a Poke ball toy, Burger King issued a $22 million recall.

Facebook

67% of United States internet users are on Facebook, while 82% of United Kingdom internet users are.

During Facebook's first summer, Mark Zuckerberg and his family spent $85,000 to keep the company afloat. He is now worth $19 billion.

There are over 70 different languages available for Facebook users, one of which is pirate.

Since Facebook launched, there have been 150 billion friend connections, 1.13 trillion likes, and 250 billion photos uploaded.

The like button was originally called the awesome button.

The average Facebook user checks their status 14 times a day.

Facebook will track what sites you visit, even after signing out.

Mark Zuckerberg is red-green color blind, which is why Facebook is mainly blue.

There are over 30 million dead people on Facebook.

1/3 of all divorces in the United States contain the word Facebook.

Facebook pays $500 to anyone that can successfully hack it.

Approximately 20% of photos taken every year end up on Facebook.

Iceland used Facebook to change their constitution in 2010.

If Facebook was a country, it would have the 3rd most populated country in the world.

Dr. Seuss

Dr. Seuss was married twice but never had any children.

Dr. Seuss wrote "Green Eggs and Ham" on a dare from his editor that he couldn't write a book using only 50 words. He did, and the words are: a, am, and, anywhere, are, be, boat, box, car, could, dark, do, eat, egg, fox, goat, good, green, ham, here, house, I, if, in, let, like, may, me, mouse, not, on, or, rain, Sam, say, see, so, thank, that , the, them, there, they, train, tree, try, will, with, would, and you.

In his lifetime, Dr. Seuss won two Academy Awards, two Emmy awards, the Pulitzer Prize, the Laura Ingles Wilder Award, and a Peabody Award.

Dr. Seuss' real name was Theodore Geisel, but some of his other pen names besides Dr. Seuss were Theo LeSieg, Rosetta Stone, and Theophrastus Suess.

The name Seuss comes from his mother's maiden name, and is also his middle name.

Seuss' first book, "And to Think I Saw It on Mulberry Street", was rejected by 27 publishers before being picked up in 1937.

Over 200,000,000 copies of Dr. Seuss' books have been sold in dozens of different languages.

Dr. Seuss drew over 400 political cartoons for the New York City paper, "PM."

Seuss owned hundreds of hats in a secret closet.

Thomas Edison

Thomas Edison's mother pulled him out of school after only 3 month after his teacher labeled him "addled" and home schooled him for the rest of his education.

Edison built his first lab in his parent's basement when he was 10 years old.

Edison would spend most of his spare money on chemicals for experiments, and to ensure that no one stole them, he labeled them all 'poison.'

Thomas Edison would pay local boys and girls a quarter each for family dogs and cats and would then electrocute the pets in public to demonstrate the dangers of alternating currents.

Thomas Edison invented the modern tattoo machine and had a mysterious tattoo on his left arm of five dots that no one knows what it meant.

Thomas Edison proposed to his wife using Morse code.

At the age of 14, Thomas Edison saved 3-year-old Jimmie MacKenzie from being hit by a boxcar. The girl's father was so thankful he taught Thomas how to be a telegraph operator.

Thomas Edison patented over 1,093 inventions in his lifetime, the last of which he filed two days before he died.

During World War 1, Thomas Edison was the head of Naval Consulting Board.

Netflix

Netflix has more subscribers than cable television in the United States.

The creator of Netflix got the idea for it after being charged a $40 late fee for a VHS copy of "Apollo 13" in 1997.

Netflix determines what TV series to pick up by looking at what is popular to download off of pirating sites.

Netflix has about 58 warehouses across the nations, but they are all hidden ad cannot be found on a map. They also disguise all of their trucks.

Netflix has an incredibly complicated algorithm to determine what movies and shows to suggest to users. According to Netflix, the hardest movie for the algorithm to suggest to users is "Napoleon Dynamite."

 Users spend over 1 billion hours per month watching Netflix.

Blockbuster had a chance to purchase Netflix for $50,000,000 in 2000, but Blockbuster just laughed.

Netflix has over 76,000 categories, including "cool mustaches," "dark Canadian thrillers," and "Understated Detective TV Shows."

The average Netflix subscriber streams 87 minutes of Netflix daily.

Netflix employees can take as many vacation days as they want.

A Netflix DVD inspector can inspect and clean up to 650 DVDs per hour, or 5,200 DVDs a day,

Elephant

Elephants are pregnant for 22-months, the longest of any land mammal.

If a member of the herd becomes sick, herd members will bring it food and help it walk.

There are only three surviving species, but it is estimated that there used to be more that forty.

Using the term Jumbo for something that is huge comes from Jumbo the elephant, who was one of the largest elephants on record, whose name comes from the Swahili word for 'boss' or 'chief.'

Elephants have the largest brain of any land mammal, at 11.023 pounds (5 kilograms).

A recent study found that elephants avoid eating from certain Acadia trees that are home to ants, as they do not want to get them in their trunks, which is lined with sensitive nerve endings.

Despite what cartoons tell you, elephants do not like peanuts. They will not eat them in the wild and zoos don't feed them to them.

Elephants will recognize themselves in the mirror.

Elephants have evolved a sixth toe.

The elephant is the only mammal that cannot jump.

At birth, an elephant calf weighs an average of 230 pounds.

The trunk of an elephant has over 40,000 muscles in it.

Elephants can't see very well.

Tongues

Like fingerprints, everyone's tongue print is different.

The world's longest tongue was 3.86 inches from the tip to the back.

The world's widest tongue was 3.1 inches wide at its widest point.

The tongue of the Blue Whale is the size of an elephant and weighs 5,400 pounds.

The world's hardest tongue twister is "The sixth sick sheikh's sixth sheep's sick."

There are over 600 different kinds of bacteria that live on a human tongue, and a millimeter of saliva contains 1,000,000 of them.

Half of the bacteria in your mouth lives on your tongue.

The tongue is the body's strongest muscle.

The tongue is the fastest healing part of the body.

The small bumps on tongues are not taste buds, but are actually papillae.

Not all taste buds are on the tongue. About 1/10 of all taste buds are found on the roof of the mouth.

In Tibet, sticking your tongue out as somebody is considered a greeting.

The average human tongue has 3,000-10,000 taste buds.

The five elements of taste perception are salty, sour, bitter, sweet, and umami.

The tongue is divided into two sections: the anterior and the posterior.

Cameras

The most expensive camera ever sold was a rare 1923 Leica camera which sold for $2.8 million.

The first disposable camera was created in 1949 and cost $1.29.

In 1990, Kodiak used plush animals in order to get kids into photography. The toys were called Kolorkins.

The largest collection of cameras is owned by Dilish Parekh, a collector since 1977. His collection has over 4,425 cameras.

The first digital camera was developed by Kodiak and was introduced in December of 1975. It weighed 8 pounds and took black and white photos.

It is estimated that over 3.8 trillion photos have been taken.

The word camera derives from the Latin word "camera obscura" meaning 'Dark Chamber.'

The oldest surviving photograph was taken in Paris in 1826. The exposure time it took for the photograph to develop was 8 hours.

There are 12 cameras on the surface of the moon, which the Apollo 11 mission had to leave behind in order to bring the extra moon rock specimens back to Earth.

George Eastman, the man who created Kodiak cameras, had a love for the letter k. He came up with the name Kodiak for his camera company with the help of his mother.

Taco Bell

There are no Taco Bells in Mexico, as it is difficult to brand in Mexico. Taco Bell's first attempt at opening chains in Mexico they branded their food as "Mexican" but customers were confused at the differences between their traditional Mexican food and Taco Bell's "Mexican" food. During their second attempt, they labeled their food "American." However, this time customers were confused by how similar their traditional food and this food. After that, Taco Bell gave up on trying to open franchises in Mexico.

The oldest Taco Bell and the oldest McDonald's are in the same town.

Taco Bell's hot sauce can be used to clean dirty pennies.

The founder of Taco Bell's name was Glen W. Bell.

The actors in Taco Bell commercials get free Taco Bell for life.

The original name of Taco Bell was Taco-Tia.

The original cost of a taco from Taco Bell was 19 cents.

The Taco Bell Chihuahua was actually a female.

One April Fool's Day, Taco Bell claimed to have purchased the Liberty Bell and were planning to rename it the Taco Liberty Bell. Outrage ensued on the US government.

At some overseas locations, Taco Bell sells french fries.

Taco Bell meat is only 88% beef.

Mount Rushmore

It took over 14 years and 400 men to complete Mount Rushmore, yet no one died on the project.

90% of Mount Rushmore was carved using dynamite. In total, over 450,000 tons of rock was removed with dynamite.

George Washington has the longest nose of anyone on the mountain, at 21 feet. The other president's noses average 20 feet long.

It is said that the first coffee break occurred during the carving of Mount Rushmore.

It total, the monument cost $989,992.32 to build.

Gutzon Borglum, the sculptor behind Mount Rushmore, was

originally commission to work on Stone Mountain in Georgia. He left on bad terms, and ended up leaving the project to Augustus Lukeman.

Borglum was a member of the Freemasons, and was possibly a member of the Ku Klux Klan.

Each day, workers had to climb more than 506 steps to get to work.

Mount Rushmore got its first cleaning in 2005. Workers spent three weeks scrubbing dirt and lichens off the monument.

There was originally going to be a secret cave behind Thomas Jefferson's head called the Hall of Records. The cave was supposed to house the story of Mount Rushmore as well as documents like the Constitution and the Declaration of Independence.

Owls

A group of owls is called a parliament, a wisdom, or a study.

Owls can turn their heads 270 degrees.

There are over 200 different species of owls.

A barn owl can eat over 1,000 mice each year.

A baby owl is known as an owlet.

The largest owl fossil ever found, Orinmegalonyx oteroi, stood over 3 feet tall.

The structure of an owl's foot is called zygodactyl.

 The smallest species of owl is the Elf Owl, which stands at around 5-6 inches tall and weigh around 1 ½ ounces.

Owl feathers are designed so that when an owl is flying, it cannot be heard. It is the only bird capable of completely silent flight.

Owls do not have teeth, so they do not chew their food.

Owls are farsighted.

The average owl lives around 20 years.

The typical owl lays three to twelve eggs in its lifetime. The eggs are round and white, and do not hatch at the same time.

Owls have an excellent sense of hearing, using ears that are located behind their eyes.

Owls have three eyelids. One for blinking, one for sleeping, and one for keeping the eye clean.

Owl eyes are round, but are tubes.

Thank you for purchasing and taking the time to read this book! If you would like to send us interesting facts, suggestions for subjects, corrections, or just questions about other books we are working on, email us at:

brant.trivia@yahoo.com

If you are interested in writing a few articles for a future project, title your email "Article Writer." If we think your articles are great, we pay between 25 cents and 1 dollar per article!

Always remember to respect
the trivia.

-Brant Entrekin

www.ingramcontent.com/pod-product-compliance
Lightning Source LLC
Chambersburg PA
CBHW020342290526
45785CB00005B/2134